THE   Watercolors

EYE   of

AND   John

THE   Stuart

HEART   Ingle

John Stuart Ingle/Photograph by Tina Barney

THE EYE AND THE HEART

Watercolors of John Stuart Ingle

INTRODUCTION BY
Frank H. Goodyear, Jr.

TEXT BY
John Camp

Rizzoli NEW YORK

IN ASSOCIATION WITH
EVANSVILLE MUSEUM OF ARTS & SCIENCE
EVANSVILLE, INDIANA

First published in the United States of America in 1988 by
Rizzoli International Publications, Inc.
597 Fifth Avenue
New York, New York 10017
in association with
Evansville Museum of Arts & Science

Produced by Chameleon Books, Inc.
211 West 20th Street
New York, New York 10011

Designed by Arnold Skolnick
Edited by Marion Wheeler
Typography by Larry Lorber, Ultracomp, New York

Production Services by Four Colour Imports, Ltd., Louisville, Kentucky
Printed and bound in Hong Kong

ISBN 0-8478-0888-2
LC 87-62204

ACKNOWLEDGMENTS

This book is the result of the collective efforts of many individuals.

We wish particularly to thank Mr. Peter Tatistcheff and Mr. Wilbur Ross of New York for lending important encouragement throughout the planning of this book and its corresponding exhibition; Marion Wheeler and Arnold Skolnick at Chameleon Books, whose enthusiasm and professional insights were an invaluable aid; the lenders from twelve states, who graciously shared works from their collections for inclusion in this book and the exhibition; and the Board of Trustees and staff of the Evansville Museum of Arts & Science—most especially presidents Jeffrey Bosse and Rita Eykamp; curator of collections Mary Schnepper; registrars Peggy Bridges and Marlene Hirsch; executive secretary Sara Nussmeier; and bookkeeper Inez Waddle, whose tireless efforts made the complex machinery of this project run smoothly.

We are most grateful to three successive Museum Guild presidents—Lisa Soelter, Martha Polk, and Julie Rang—and their respective boards and membership for generously providing major funding for this publication.

John Stuart Ingle wishes to acknowledge the support and encouragement given him by the administration, faculty, and staff of the University of Minnesota-Morris over the period of years represented by the work in this book and exhibition.

J.W.S., III

This book, which accompanies the exhibition "The Eye and the Heart: Watercolors of John Stuart Ingle," was organized by the Evansville Museum of Arts & Science and made possible by a generous grant from the Evansville Museum Guild.

DATES OF THE EXHIBITION

Wadsworth Atheneum
Hartford Connecticut
January 17–March 5, 1988

Evansville Museum of Arts & Science
Evansville, Indiana
March 20–May 8, 1988

Hunter Museum of Art
Chattanooga, Tennessee
May 29–July 24, 1988

Mitchell Museum
Mt. Vernon, Illinois
August 14–October 9, 1988

Springfield Art Museum
Springfield, Missouri
October 30, 1988–January 1, 1989

University Art Museum, University of Minnesota
Minneapolis, Minnesota
January 21–March 12, 1989

CONTENTS

FOREWORD

It was in a church pew in 1975 that I first heard John Stuart Ingle's name. I had recently arrived in Evansville to become director of the museum, and the name was introduced to me in a whisper by a proud mother. She told me that her son was a painter—and a good one. In a scenario not unfamiliar to anyone in my profession, we both smiled and nodded, after this murmured confidence, and then sang a hymn.

I do not recall any mention of Ingle's name again until I read a review six years later by *New York Times'* critic Hilton Kramer in which he referred to John Stuart Ingle as "something of a discovery." Mrs. Ingle had been right.

In 1982, I visited the Tatistcheff Gallery in New York to see Ingle's work firsthand. By then, the artist's success was such that no paintings were readily available, but Peter Tatistcheff kindly arranged for me to see a recently completed work in a private collection. Still unframed, it was *Study for Still Life with Brass Candlestick*. Nothing I had seen in reproduction prepared me for the luminous, transcendent quality of a painting by Ingle. Although the painting measures only eleven-by-fourteen inches, its impact is epic.

Not long after the visit to New York, we began laying the groundwork for John Stuart Ingle's first major retrospective exhibition. This book and an insightful video documentary by the Indiana filmmaker Calvin Kimbrough have been produced in conjunction with the exhibition, all of which, we hope, will extend to a wider public the pleasure of discovering the treasures that Ingle's eye and heart have so vividly informed.

John W. Streetman, III
Director
Evansville Museum of Arts & Science

A Word from the Artist

At the beginning of 1975, there was a dramatic change of style and expressive content in my painting. It was the result of a small civil war that had taken place the year before. The product of this change has been a long and continuing series of watercolors; almost all of them are still lifes.

Prior to 1975, I painted a series of acrylics which were non-figurative, geometric color studies. As a sort of *violon d'Ingres,* I also worked on a series of watercolor landscapes. These were broad-gestured images done in a rather loose, spontaneous style. I thought of them as realizations of the essence of the landscape, an essence that was a vivid spatial configuration. To realize this essence with force, I needed, I thought, to minimize the importance of the individual things in the landscape by minimizing their description.

Early in 1974, I was disconcerted to find that my feelings about the landscape began to change. The vividly glowing and tactile presence of the things in nature began to force itself upon my imagination and into my paintings. For an uncomfortable few months, my watercolors were a battleground witnessing a struggle between two incompatible ways of seeing.

With time, the force of my new feelings gathered strength and overwhelmed my old concern for the spatial essence of the landscape. By the end of the year, I had pretty well defined a new direction for my painting, one which replaced the direction taken in painting the nonfigurative acrylics as well as the landscapes.

As 1975 began, I was at work on the first painting of my new direction. It was a watercolor still life, and in it I strove to realize, as fully as possible, the extraordinarily vivid and tactile presence of things seen in a certain way. Twelve years later, I am still at it.

John Stuart Ingle
Morris, Minnesota

INTRODUCTION

A child said, What is the grass? fetching it to me with
    full hands;
How could I answer the child?…I do not know what it
    is any more than he.

                  (Walt Whitman, *Leaves of Grass*, 1855)

John Stuart Ingle's work reverberates with art historical associations, none of which is insistently predominant. There is, of course, the obvious visual link with the great traditions of seventeenth-century Dutch still-life painting. The incessant reality of things, a childlike wonderment and fascination with everyday and exotic objects, and a concomitant symbolism, more personal and idiosyncratic in Ingle's case than in his Dutch predecessors, dominates Ingle's vision. That vision finds reenforcement in the still lifes of the nineteenth-century American painter John Frederick Peto, although Peto's touch is far more French than Ingle's. Finally, it is in the abstraction of twentieth-century art that Ingle's work finds its measure. As in the late paintings of Piet Mondrian, there is a dynamic equilibrium between shapes and colors concealed by a realist's vision that controls the naturalness apparent in Ingle's compositions. The precision in Ingle's measure is an inherent factor in the artist's overall decision making process; nothing is arbitrary in John Stuart Ingle's art.

In the final analysis, however, focusing on the associative links with art history and other artists directs attention away from the real meaning of Ingle's work. That real meaning, it seems to me, is the artist's serious commitment to understand the physical world and his own relationship to it through the making of art. Ingle's paintings are for him what Walden Pond was for Henry David Thoreau—a means leading to self-awareness and knowledge.

Ingle's commitment, like Thoreau's, far exceeds the goal of mere description of the "objectness" of the physical world. Certainly, the process of object selection, what he's going to paint, is of vital importance as is his description of the objects, but the ultimate irony of Ingle's work is that the process and the resultant literalness speak to means not ends. One can imagine Ingle agreeing wholeheartedly with Walt Whitman's lines in *Leaves of Grass*: "The facts are useful and real…they are not my dwelling…I enter by them to an area of the dwelling."

It would seem that Ingle's claims to knowledge, his ultimate "dwelling," are both non-Christian and non-scientific. They are personal claims, motivated by personal needs, acted out through the experience of repetition. His watercolors, solitary fragments of knowledge, make no claim, neither singly nor as a body of work, to completeness in describing reality or the artist's own awareness. They are marks on a yardstick of human experience, made along the way, that measure Ingle's own struggles with understanding reality. As Ralph Waldo Emerson wrote, somewhat despairingly, "To know a little, would be worth the expense of this world."

What is John Stuart Ingle's place in contemporary American art? Like other contemporary American realists, artists like Sondra Freckelton, Carolyn Brady, and James Valerio, who also paint tabletop still lifes, Ingle delights in giving the viewer a lot to look at. While not a photorealist, although he does use the airbrush techniques of photorealism, his finished watercolors do evince the incredible technical virtuosity of photorealism. This passion for putting down on paper everything that can be seen, for gathering data and recording it, is an historic condition and, thus, has been viewed in some contemporary critical circles as anachronistic and lacking in legitimacy. Ingle's work, like the best work of the contemporary realists, reflects upon its contemporaniety; it is a product of contemporary life, shaped by the forces that make contemporary life unique from other times. The factors of time, place, and personality shape all of our lives. John Stuart Ingle is no exception. Removed from the babble that defines so much of the contemporary art world, he is able to forge remarkable images that challenge our perceptions of life, forcing us to ask the question, as the child did, "What is the grass?"

Frank H. Goodyear, Jr.
President
Pennsylvania Academy of the Fine Arts

THE Watercolors

EYE of

AND John

THE Stuart

HEART Ingle

A MAN IN A LANDSCAPE

John Stuart Ingle paints still-life watercolors of golden-ripe pears and deep-red strawberries, antique tables and hand-thrown pots, crystal bowls and lace doilies, and cold-steel paring knives, oriental carpets, arabesque tile, and gourmet candies as real as small children.

His works have an astonishing sensuality and a riveting immediacy. They are created in the most homely of circumstances, in a light- and plant-filled studio on a shady side street in Morris, Minnesota.

Morris nestles in comfortable isolation on the eastern rim of the great prairie, one-hundred-and-fifty miles west of the Twin Cities. The countryside around the town is filled with life of stunning variety and color: ivory-billed coots paddle across the frequent small ponds, beneath red-winged and yellow-headed blackbirds perched in the cattails. Cylindrical bales of hay glow butter-yellow against deep green fields of alfalfa. Black-and-white dairy cows wander placidly through pastures, chewing their cuds and peering with zenlike calm at passing cars. Orange-bellied bluebirds, purple martins, and juncos perch on roadside powerlines. Silver-blue Russian olives march along fencerows, and towering lightning-struck cottonwoods mark the farmsites.

Morris is typical of the small Midwestern farming villages built along the agricultural frontier of the late nineteenth century. At one end of the main street, which is lined with tan- and red-brick business facades, a grain elevator stands, at the other, a convenience store. Throughout the town, white clapboard homes are built on low, gently rolling hills, along blacktopped streets shaded by elms and maples, and vegetable patches peek from behind board fences. On warm summer days, cloud-fresh laundry hangs from backyard clotheslines, and children play hopscotch on cracked concrete sidewalks. Calvary Cemetery, its fading limestone gravemarkers brooding among dark pines, adds a poetical ambience—and provides a convenient, if somewhat spooky, rendezvous on warm evenings for amorous undergraduates from the town's college.

The University of Minnesota-Morris is unusual. The state set out to create a traditional, small-town brick-and-ivy liberal arts school. Against all odds, it succeeded.

It was the college that attracted John Stuart Ingle, when he was offered a job there as a painting instructor in 1966. At that time, after three years in graduate school at the University of Arizona, Ingle was painting abstractions in oil or acrylic, focusing on the physical and psychological effects of color. He continued that work at Morris.

He also did something else. Almost as an exercise, as a pianist plays scales, Ingle went into the countryside to paint realistic landscapes in watercolor. ("But not quite like that, like a pianist doing scales," Ingle comments, consistent with his belief that everything important is immensely complicated, and thus, analogies are never quite accurate.)

When Ingle began to paint them, the landscapes were brushed out in the wide, loose gesture of most contemporary watercolors. Eventually, that style no longer served his purpose. The more Ingle painted landscapes, the more it seemed to him that his paintings were really about color and paper, not about the large-scale world around him. If there was a secret to be revealed, it was not in the broad form or loose gesture of landscapes, but in the detailed, more defined elements of nature—in the leaves on the trees, the pebbles in a stream bed, and blades of grass. And the exquisite and inescapable presence of these sensual textures are revealed most clearly in Minnesota's northern light.

In the summer, there are times when the soft, moist air from the Gulf of Mexico creeps into Minnesota. On the nights when it does, fireflies illuminate roadside ditches, and you can lie in bed and hear the corn grow. During the day, the land takes on the soft, impressionist glow of the Midi. But usually the light in Minnesota is unmistakably northern: sharp and defining. A hillside of red oak is precisely that, not maple or elm or sumac. A field of soybean may glow golden brown in the autumn sun, as does a field of corn, but the northern light reveals one as soybean, the other as corn, and they are no more alike than the Mississippi and the Hudson rivers.

The texture of the countryside, Ingle has said, began to impress itself upon him. The pressure was not violent, but it was insistent. Almost against his will, he responded and began to explore the world of detail and texture.

As it happened, Ingle's exploration took him out of the Morris countryside into the realm of still life, painted in the studio. That his work should focus on still life, and not landscape, was adventitious. Ingle's subject matter might have remained landscape, or he might have chosen the figure, or even portraiture but for the countryside—the landscape in and around Morris—which made it necessary, even unavoidable, for him to choose to describe objective reality more intimately.

A Necessary Analogy

Some art demands an accompanying text to render it comprehensible. Ingle's art does not. It requires viewers not words.

In conversation, Ingle refers to his paintings as "reports" or "investigations." His reports are not painted by chance, training, preference, convenience, tradition, or because painting is his only skill. He is an exceptional photographer and a most literate man with the requisite skills to make his reports either photographically or in written form, but Ingle makes his reports in paint because paint is the only medium that permits him to properly explore his chosen subject. Paint is not an option, but a necessity. That necessity can best be explained by analogy.

Suppose you wished to take a vacation trip to the territory of Ingle's childhood, which is located in the Ohio Valley where Indiana and Illinois look across the river to Kentucky.

The geography of the area is complicated by three state highway systems and two major rivers. Large, cluttered metropolitan areas are separated by lonely stretches of rural countryside. The dividing line between the Eastern and Central time zones meanders through the landscape; a gravel road or a back fenceline may, and often does, separate Eastern clocks from their siblings in the Midwest.

To deal with these complications, a tourist might buy a guidebook, read some history, or talk to friends who had traveled there. Almost any traveler would obtain a roadmap.

A map of the region represents particular kinds of information simply and clearly. It shows the shape of things: how the Ohio River slashes through the countryside, where it meets the Wabash, and where the bridges and towns are located. If one thinks for a moment about the information displayed on a road map, it quickly becomes apparent that no text or guidebook can duplicate the map's essential function. A map is a visual representation of a spacial reality. Its essence is shape and symbol.

The same is true of Ingle's work. No text or guide can duplicate the essential function of the paintings. To write that an apple painted by Ingle is red and realistic is to say that Renoir painted pretty young girls. Both statements are true but certainly not the whole truth.

But now the analogy between a roadmap and painting by John Stuart Ingle no longer serves. Analogies "never quite work," and this analogy is no exception. A map is a *simplified* version of reality, but a painting by Ingle is as *complicated as its subjects.*

When Ingle paints apples in a bowl, he is exploring the nature of human psychology and perception, as well as the form and substance of a group of physical objects, and graphically presenting his findings.

If words are inadequate to describe the content of a map, neither can words alone reveal the myriad findings reported in a painting by Ingle. To say that words alone cannot adequately describe Ingle's work is not to argue, however, that words are useless. They are useful in other ways. Biography is one of them.

A Brief Biography

John Stuart Ingle was born two blocks from the Ohio River in Evansville, Indiana, in 1933. He was the younger of two sons in a prosperous mercantile and mining family whose roots in Evansville go back several generations.

> *Viewed through the faulty optics of memory, my childhood looks like Tom Sawyer's and Huck Finn's. It was absolutely magical. On weekends, my Uncle John would take my brother and me on cruises up the Ohio, up to Duck Island. People went there to picnic and to swim. The memories of those times and places are still very vivid, very tactile: the overgrown trees, the sound of people laughing and playing, the smell of the river and river mud…it's vivid stuff.*

The first years of Ingle's life were spent in a fine upper-middle-class neighborhood "with yellow-brick streets and big white houses," and always the Ohio River, just a street away and across a park. Family, too, was close by. One set of grandparents lived across the street, the other, next door.

Ingle's parents were members of the Evansville social circle that involved itself with the arts. They were active in the museum, and Ingle's mother, Susan, was involved with the Evansville Symphony, wrote poetry, and maintained a serious interest in the theater. His father, David, an engineer, was an excellent draughtsman. His father's brother, Thomas Ingle, was a professional painter who taught art at Connecticut College.

When professional artists came to town, they might well have stopped at the Ingles' and talked to John: "I was given to understand at a young age that I had some substantial talent in art. By the time I was ten, I was adamant about the idea of being an artist," Ingle said.

Magical as his childhood might have been, it was not uniformly happy. His parents were divorced when Ingle was six, just before World War II. During the war, his father served overseas in the military, and his mother went to work in an ammunition plant. After a short time, she fell ill and was hospitalized in Evansville for nearly a year. Eventually she was diagnosed as having tuberculosis, and it was suggested that she move to Tucson, Arizona, where the dry climate was believed to be curative.

John Ingle and his older brother, David, moved to Tucson with their mother. While she was undergoing treatment for a year, the brothers boarded at the Southern Arizona School for Boys. The following year, David returned to Evansville to live with his father, while John remained in Arizona and attended the Greenfield School for Boys. It was there that he received his first formal art instruction.

The Greenfield School "was an invaluable experience," he said, "the type of place where you learn how to learn." He remained at the school through the tenth grade and then transferred to the Tucson public high school. The public school, he said, was a waste of his time.

When Susan Ingle had recovered enough to set up housekeeping in Tucson, she arranged for intensive precollege tutoring for John, and he dropped out of high school. He scored well on ACT tests and at age fifteen entered the University of Arizona where he studied for four years, taking all the arts courses necessary for a Bachelor of Fine Arts, without actually getting the degree. "I didn't get it because I didn't take the other courses you needed, like foreign languages. They didn't interest me," Ingle said.

In 1953, after he left the university, he and his mother moved back to Evansville. Ingle worked for a year and made some money painting portraits. In 1954, he and his mother decided to tour Europe. "We went to France and we planned to go to Italy, but wound up going to Spain, instead, because you could live there so cheaply," Ingle recalls. "It was so cheap it was ridiculous."

Eventually they arrived at Majorca to stay in what he says was "probably the ugliest little town on the island...but we had a beautiful villa on the Mediterranean."

On Majorca, Ingle spent a good deal of time at a beach hotel. One day he was at the hotel playing a desultory game of chess with the bartender, when a woman came in. The regular desk clerk was away, so the bartender tried to help her. As it happened, the bartender could speak only Spanish, and she could speak only English and French. The woman was attractive, Ingle said, and he quickly volunteered to interpret.

The woman was Germaine (Gigi) Zeghers, a Belgian tourist. In a story line that might have been lifted from a movie, she and Ingle fell in love. In 1956, they were married.

Gigi came from Brussels, and it was there that they went to live. Ingle supported himself and his new wife by painting decorative works marketed through department stores. He does not now consider the work of those years to be particularly interesting. It was, he said, a form of craftsmanship.

I don't deny it, and it did prove interesting in one way: I demonstrated to myself that I could earn my living with my hands, so to speak. I have the facility to earn some kind of living as a painter-craftsman. That's a valuable thing to know about yourself. I'm not interested in doing that anymore, and I'm not very interested in that work; but I don't deny it.

After eight years in Brussels, Ingle made one of the sudden turns that have marked his life.

About 1963, about the time I turned thirty, I conceived the idea that I should take a more active and responsible attitude toward the world. Eventually I decided to become a teacher. That meant I had to return to the U.S. and finish my degree.

Ingle returned to the University of Arizona and completed the requirements for a Bachelor of Fine Arts degree in 1964. In 1966, he received a Master of Fine Arts degree.

"I was offered a job as a painting instructor in Morris, and I took it, and here I am." Ingle is now a full professor of studio art. He and Gigi have two grown children, Colette and David.

The Evolution of a Style

Ingle's early training at the University of Arizona emphasized traditional artistic skills. He was given a strong grounding in drawing, design, perspective, and anatomy, training he now believes to be invaluable. "Those tools are among a student's essential acquisitions," Ingle commented. "They produce whatever amount of facility a student might have. Whatever facility I have can be traced to that discipline." He is adamant about the value of traditional training after teaching art for more than two decades:

> *The value of academic training to someone who will do something quite different—stripe paintings or other totally nonobjective work—is that it develops a sensitivity to nuances of pattern, shape, and interval. Proportional relationships are relevant to the drawing of meaningful images of all kinds, whether or not they are descriptive in the obvious sense.*

Furthermore, he argues, academic discipline may be the only effective way to teach and to be taught:

> *Drawing can't be taught intellectually, in a linear-verbal way. It must be taught in some other way, yet students must be given some kind of feedback on the success or failure of their efforts. If a student says, "This image in my head is a real stunner, can you help me produce it?" I have to say, "No," because I don't know what it is, and the student can't tell me.*

> *If the student is drawing a classical cast, I can say that the nose is too long or the shadows are too heavy, and I think we can come to some reasonable agreement on how the student has represented the cast. The student may not be very interested in drawing a cast, but an artist will find it extremely valuable to have the analytical abilities to do it.*

Although his training was solid, Ingle did not hit upon a line of exploration that felt genuinely compelling. When he moved to Morris, as an instructor, he was experimenting with color. "The work was abstract, very geometrical. I was trying to learn more about color. Not color for this purpose or that purpose, but just how colors felt," he recalls.

He produced enough paintings for an exhibition, but, at the same time, he was getting in trouble on another front.

> *I pursued that abstract style from about 1966 to about 1974. While I was*

doing all the color work, the abstract work, I was painting those water-color landscapes as a change of pace. I don't know...intuitively, I thought it was an important activity. It felt creative, like it was going somewhere.

The problem—and this was a real problem that I struggled with, worried about constantly—was that I found my style changing to a more textured and meticulous view of the world. I found myself wondering about the style of the leaves on trees, or the ways of representing the tops of bare trees as you see them on a hillside.

The upshot of that work, the landscapes, was that I decided to do a series of paintings that would clarify the problem of texture. I thought I would be doing things like figures and landscapes in oil or acrylics. I wound up doing still lifes in watercolor purely through circumstance.

It was winter, over Christmas break, when you can't paint outside here and I didn't have the facilities at home for elaborate figure work in oils. And it was the holiday season and a lot was going on. So I set up a still life and did it in watercolor. Somewhat to my surprise, I found that it was quite a satisfactory arena for what I wanted to do—both the medium of watercolor and the subject of still life.

Notes On Technique

Ingle paints the objects of a daily life, although perhaps not the daily life of just anyone. They are, rather, the objects that might surround someone of American origin from a specifically Midwestern upper-middle-class background—someone who, like Ingle, might come from a comfortable mercantile family in Evansville or Cincinnati or St. Louis or St. Paul.

He paints the lushest of orchids, the cattleya, set beside the brassiest of house plants, the geranium. He paints ripening pears or strawberries and oriental rugs. He paints old silver and cut glass on fine antique tables. He paints chocolate candies imported from Belgium. He has been doing this, since Christmas 1974.

And he does it very carefully. Each painting takes weeks or months to complete. The still life is painstakingly arranged, observed inter-minably, and painted with an obsessive intensity.

The scale that I prefer is slightly larger than life, but not so much larger as to seem bloated or gigantic. I'd prefer that most people not be conscious that the painting is larger than life. I use scale to emphasize the importance of the experience that the painting represents.

Ingle argues that the way most people experience reality depends to a large extent on their frame of mind. He had that intuition one night while watching television. An objectionable commercial came on, he remembers, and he turned his head away, looking into a darker part of the room. His eye retained an after-image of the television screen, and he was astounded by its small size.

The after-image was the size of a postage stamp. Literally. I realized that if you held a postage stamp out at the distance you would to read it, it would be about the same size as a television screen seen across the room.

I thought that was bizarre. I had been pulled into the action of a movie, and had read life-size into that postage-stamp-size visual experience. I realized that things seem bigger when you focus on them. I realized I could use that to impress a viewer with the results of a highly concentrated awareness.

And that is what he is reporting upon in all his work: awareness. Good paintings are nothing less than models of understanding.

I have less trust in intellectual knowledge than I do of immediate experience. I don't think that "thinking things through" is necessarily the powerful tool we usually profess it to be.

No doubt experts could measure all the components of a baseball player hitting a ball and could predict where the ball would land, but it would take them forever. A good fielder can do that without thinking about it.

You can find all the evidence you want that our processes of knowing are much more fragile than we prefer to believe. I would say that the baseball player who, at the crack of the bat, proceeds in the right direction and makes a full speed, arm-outstretched catch represents the use of a kind of knowledge or wisdom not available through intellectual inspection. That's the kind of knowledge I'm trying to investigate, and report upon.

The Artist's Tools

Ingle makes most of his reports on 300- and 400-pound white d'Arches watercolor paper mounted (for painting) on a particle-board backing with masking tape. His paints are soft tube-type watercolors made by Winsor & Newton of London, England. Small or delicate work is done with black-handled sable brushes of several brands, most generally the well-known Winsor & Newton Series 7.*

Large washes are done with several sizes of flat wash brushes or with two soft-haired Chinese watercolor brushes wired together to form a single brush. Ingle also makes rare use of a Paasche AB airbrush to place extremely delicate layers of paint on specific areas where the touch of a brush or too much water might disturb the underlying color.

The paintings themselves are blocked out with a mechanical drawing pencil on an expansive professional drafting table. The largest of his paintings to date are about forty by sixty inches, the size of the largest available sheet of d'Arches 300-pound watercolor paper.

Ingle is an expert photographer and makes what might be called photographic notations of his compositions, especially those that include perishables. The photographs are made with a Sinar view camera to capture the detail provided by large format negatives—the Sinar can handle anything up to an eight-by-ten inch negative. A Nikon 35mm single-lens reflex camera is used for more casual notations. Ingle's reasons

---

*He is extremely sensitive to the feel and response of his brushes and works with several different styles and brands. He was most annoyed when he decided that the famed Series 7 quality had fallen; and he was most pleased by what he felt was the brand's later recovery.

for using his camera are complex:

> *I'm interested in photography, but my paintings don't have much to do with photorealism. The photorealists, as I understand them, are interested in reproducing the qualities of a photograph. I'm not content with the qualities of photographs.*

> *In a drawing or painting, you have a record of a certain space through time. It has a tactile quality that gets at the softness of surfaces. It gives you a record of a visual experience that's informed by a lot of intuition about the way things are. You don't have that with a camera, and as a result you get a kind of space that has a fixed flatness.*

> *I use a camera as a tool. If it weren't for the camera, I'd have to do a lot of painstaking but really pretty routine drawings, just figuring things out. A photograph is a reasonable and useful instrument for investigation, but certainly not the primary one. It can also be a treacherous instrument. I never, never trust the color in a photograph.**

Ingle's facility with his tools and materials—the brushes and paint and sparkling white paper—has produced a series of watercolors of spectacular reality. So striking is his technique that it attracts very intense attention by first-time critics and viewers, causing Ingle to be concerned about their reactions.

> *My greatest anxiety is that nobody will see past the technique, but at this point, after some experience at watching people look at my work, and reading some critics, I'm content that most people do get past it. People let me know what they think about the technique, but they also let me know that something else has touched them.*

---

*Ingle's use of a camera is made more interesting because of his draughting skill. He often sends sketches of proposed watercolors to his New York dealer, a fact noted by Kenneth Baker in his article, "New American Watercolor," in *Portfolio* magazine. Baker states that the high degree of finish in Ingle's paintings is clearly a conscious strategy, because those preliminary sketches are as "brisk, effortless, and lyrical" as the final works are refined.

Ingle's Place in American Painting

To understand Ingle's place in American art, it is necessary to look back three decades. When he was an undergraduate at the University of Arizona, the New York School's experimentation in abstract expressionism, which culminated in the work of artists such as Jackson Pollock, Franz Kline and Willem de Kooning, was sweeping the country. Theories conceived by modernist critics—Clement Greenberg, for one—were hotly argued everywhere, but the triumph of modernism had not yet been fully accepted in most art schools. Ingle, therefore, received a conventional and very thorough grounding in the traditional skills. At a time when the rising stars of the art world debated the value of academic training, Ingle was drawing plaster casts and learning the Latin names for muscles.

And, as the second wave of postwar modernism rose in New York—and, indeed, as American critics began to claim with confidence that the center of world art had shifted from Europe to America—Ingle shifted himself from America to Europe.

In his nine-year stay there, Ingle, ever the curious intellectual, was profoundly aware of developments in the new art. At the same time, he found himself surrounded by masterpieces of seventeenth-century lowland still life—still life so powerful that it could not be ignored.*

When Ingle returned to the United States, his purely modernist impulses held the upper hand for a while. At the time he finished his graduate work, he was immersed in a formal study of color and color effects, producing nonobjective paintings strongly influenced by the colorist Josef Albers, and he worked intently along those lines for several years. Then came the break and the beginning of his exploration of the

---

*In a *New York Times* review of an exhibition of Ingle's work at the Tatistcheff Gallery, New York, critic Hilton Kramer commented on the influence of seventeenth-century Dutch painting on Ingle's work. Kramer, now editor of the influential art journal, *The New Criterion,* found Ingle possessed "of a mature talent and formidable technique, a worthy successor to the seventeenth-century Dutch still-life painters who have provided his art with its essential precedents of style."

world of external reality, which continues.

It is important to understand that, while his current work is richly representational, it is substantially affected, nevertheless, by the geometrical and colorist abstractions on which he spent so many years. Ingle does not use design as explicitly as an abstractionist might, but neither does he push it as deeply into the background as an Old Master. In Ingle's paintings, the design rides the surface of the painting as firmly as the objects. He is, in that sense, a very modern realist, a hybrid that a few decades back might have been considered impossible.*

Although Ingle is firmly modern and his paintings are easily at home in the late twentieth century, he is not particularly interested in commenting on the media-saturated, mass-production society that America has become, as are the pop artists and the photorealists.

His paintings resolutely turn away from current fashion and mass production. In *Colonel Charles Denby's Desk* (1985), a painting which contains that most ubiquitous of mass-produced items, a roll of postage stamps, the stamps are glimpsed within an elaborately decorated antique stamp dispenser.

Ingle has no interest in telling stories, nor in evoking the kind of sentimentalism or nostalgia generated by renderings of antique objects and fading pre-war Americana—crumbling red barns, decrepit wheelbarrows, and black Model A Fords rusting among goldenrod and thistles. Nor do his paintings contain obvious political or social commentary: no causes are promoted or defended. He is, in truth, a singlularly independent artist, claiming that he is "of no school or party, and has no wish to join one."

---

*In the past few years, Ingle has departed only once from his general subject matter of still life. The departure came in a portrait commission, which he accepted not quite on whimsy, but in a certain lighthearted spirit, to see what would happen. What resulted was a lengthy struggle, almost bitter in its intensity, ending with a painting reminiscent of Degas' family portraits. The subject matter of this painting is rather conventional—an obviously well-to-do family consisting of a husband and wife, a son and a daughter, and some antique furniture in what might once have been called a drawing room—but the arrangement of the forms is so magical that it transcends its genre. More than a family portrait and less, the painting is beautifully balanced within a subtle amalgam of line, color, figures, and objects that defies a linear, literal interpretation.

If Ingle's paintings are "about" anything, they are about Reality—the same Reality that inspired the great seventeenth-century philosophers and today's young generation of particle and quantum physicists. Like the philosophers and the scientists, Ingle is conducting an intellectual inquiry into the nature of external reality and observation, and provides a uniquely intense accumulation of information about the observable world in his work. He is even quite scientific about it in his own artist's way: "I dont *want* to make arbitrary changes in what I see to paint the picture, I want to paint what is *given*. The whole idea is to take something that's given and explore that reality as intensely as I can."

The Man behind the Words—And the Woman

A personal chronology reveals a lot about an artist, but not everything. And Ingle is a tricky subject.

John Ingle is a tallish, slender man with a receding hairline and neatly trimmed mustache. His working dress runs to pullover shirts and corduroy slacks. Asked a question that he takes seriously, he usually will mull it over before venturing to answer it. When he does, he speaks deliberately in complete sentences.

To see Ingle in his small town among his plants, taking his solitary ten-minute walks from home to work, shopping in one of the town's three supermarkets, baking bread in his well-appointed kitchen, or conversing with his colleagues at the college, one is struck by the simplicity and tranquility of his life. And yet, on closer look, he is clearly a man of great intensity and determination, working under a substantial amount of self-imposed stress.

Before he begins a painting, several criteria must be met: the subject must be intrinsically interesting; design and color must work perfectly; and the actual work of creating the painting must serve to advance his research. Painting is never easy to Ingle.

"When he's starting a painting, he's terrible, and he's getting worse," his wife, Gigi, declared. "He moves furniture around and takes things out of the cabinets and cupboards and linen closets and the bookcases. And then he starts looking for something that he knows we have and he can't find it, and he goes through everything. This goes on for days."

Ingle's studio is a big, airy room built on the back of his home. He works with classical music playing, surrounded by plants, most notably several large, lush cattleyas, the most spectacular of orchids. When he is not working, he prepares complex dishes for lunches and dinners, featuring his homemade bread, that are served in simple, casual comfort. Something always smells good in Ingle's house.

The walls of his home are decorated with his own paintings and those given to him by other artists. Bookcases are crammed with a variety of fiction and nonfiction, including a large collection of cookbooks. There are Oriental carpets on the floors, and the elaborately tiled kitchen is filled with antique furniture, hand-thrown pots, and dozens of small wooden and ceramic items picked up at farm auctions and estate sales.

Ingle deliberately surrounds himself with things that appeal immediately to the senses: his environment vibrates with variety and texture, line and color, and soft and hard surfaces.

Although she denies having much to do with his paintings, Gigi is an important presence in Ingle's working environment. When selecting objects for his compositions, Ingle seeks a certain feel, an aura that clicks pictorially for him. His home is filled with candidates. Most of them, as it happens, have been collected by his wife.

> Once I did a painting, quite a nice painting, that had a Red Wing crock in it. We got an immediate call about it. It was a woman from Iowa. She wasn't interested in buying the painting, but did want to make an offer on the crocks. If I knew back then what I know now, I'd have had Gigi out shopping every day. Everything she has bought is worth several times what we paid for it. Those crocks cost $20 a piece, and we've been offered $250 for them.

Gigi also arranges the flowers for his paintings. Ingle could probably do it—although he credits Gigi with a special talent—but does not.

"You've got to be careful about art. Flower arranging is an art, and I don't want to get into it. I want to paint what it given."

Ingle says flatly that his working life is often intensely uncomfortable. He speaks of paintings as imposing themselves upon him. He speaks of being forced in particular directions, quite against his will. He speaks of the cruelty of the moment when he realizes that a particular painting will fail to resolve all the questions he has raised in its conception and execution.

> *You know, intellectually, that no painting is going to do everything, but emotionally, you keep hoping. It's like hoping your child will become the President of the United States and trying not to be disappointed when he only turns out to be a governor.*

As intellectually uncomfortable as he often finds himself, he admits that he would probably not be happy doing anything else. He likes the life of the artist. He also likes how and where he lives.

> *Morris is a comfortable place to live. I like it here. I like to work here, I like the people, and I like my colleagues. We probably have the only truly collegial art department on the face of the earth. I love to go to an opening in New York and have people say nice things and go around to the restaurants and galleries and so on, but it's also nice to come back here and walk down the street at night and somebody says, "Who is that?" and then they say, "Oh, it's only you."*

> *You don't have city problems here. You don't have to drive a half hour to get to work and spend fifteen minutes looking for a place to park. It doesn't take fifteen minutes to drive to the grocery store. Here in Morris I can drive to the store, and, when I get out of the car, I open the trunk and go into the store and buy groceries and come out and the trunk is open...I'm saying you don't have to worry about things like personal security here. There's an ease to living in a town like this that allows you to focus on your work.*

> *Cities have distractions, like restaurants. I could go to a good new restaurant every night of my life, and, if I lived in New York, I might find myself doing exactly that. What would happen to my work?*

Future Work

Ingle will continue to paint watercolor still life. As of now, he is satisfied with the creative progress that has enabled him to learn to observe and to communicate his observations to his viewers.

Close readers of this brief text may notice that a pattern of cycles marks Ingle's life, each about a decade long, and that each cycle has been preceeded by a distinct change of direction.

He lived in Midwestern Evansville for ten years, moving then to Tucson for ten years. After a brief stay in the Midwest, he lived in Europe for nine years—his "craftsman" period. Then it was back to America and, once again, the Midwest, to a decade of intense work in color and abstract forms. In 1974 he began painting still life. According to his past history, Ingle should be ripe for another change of direction.

Ingle believes that the current revival of realism in American painting will eventually culminate in large multifigured works that are fully informed by modernism and embrace the many wildly disparate tendencies in this era of artistic pluralism.

John Stuart Ingle is an artist of considerable talent and a man with a sense of purpose. One suspects that when the culmination occurs, he intends to be there.

John Camp

The Watercolors

STILL LIFE WITH VERMEER
1980
60 × 40 inches
Philip Morris Companies Inc.

STILL LIFE WITH CAKE BOX
1980
60 × 40 inches
Becton Dickinson and Company
Franklin Lakes, New Jersey

(overleaf)

STILL LIFE WITH RED COSMOS
1980
45½ × 40 inches
Private Collection

STILL LIFE WITH GILDED PLATE
1980
44 × 32 inches
Shearson Lehman Brothers
New York

STILL LIFE WITH TANGERINES AND CINNAMON STICKS
1981
40 × 60 inches
Mr. and Mrs. Marco Grassi
New York

(overleaf)

STILL LIFE WITH RED WING CROCKS
1980
40 × 60 inches
Yale University Art Gallery, Gift of
Mr. Wilson Nolen, B.A. 1948, and Mrs. Nolen

STILL LIFE WITH HOLLYHOCKS AND PEARS
1981
49 × 36½ inches
Barbara and Donald Tober
New York

STUDY FOR STILL LIFE WITH GLADIOLI
1981
20 × 14½ inches
Janice C. Oresman
New York

(overleaf)

STILL LIFE WITH ROSEWOOD TABLE
1982
60 × 40 inches
Barbara and Donald Tober
New York

STILL LIFE WITH WATERMELON
1982
60 × 40 inches
Stephen S. Alpert

STILL LIFE WITH SILVER TEAPOT
1982
30 × 40 inches
Dr. John J. Weber
New York

(overleaf)

STILL LIFE WITH OVERLAND FLYER
1982
60 × 40 inches
Tatistcheff Gallery
New York

STILL LIFE WITH BRASS CANDLESTICK
1982
29½ × 42 inches
The Metropolitan Museum of Art
Gift of Dr. and Mrs. Robert E. Carroll, 1984

STILL LIFE WITH TEA CADDY
1982
40 × 30 inches
Mr. and Mrs. Barney A. Ebsworth

STUDY FOR STILL LIFE WITH BRASS CANDLESTICK
1982
11 × 14 inches
Private Collection
(not pictured)

(overleaf)

STUDY FOR STILL LIFE WITH TEA CADDY
1982
16¼ × 13 inches
Mr. and Mrs. Walter P. Fekula
New York
(not pictured)

STUDY FOR GRAND CATTLEYA
1983
14 × 21 inches
Judith and Wilbur L. Ross, Jr.
New York

STILL LIFE WITH MINIATURE GERANIUM AND SILVER QUARTER
1983
22½ × 17 inches
Mr. and Mrs. Leonidas D. Deters, Jr.
Louisville, Kentucky

STUDY FOR STILL LIFE WITH EIGHT TULIPS
1983
19¼ × 13¾ inches
Citizens National Bank
Evansville, Indiana

STILL LIFE WITH NINE TULIPS
1983
40 × 60 inches
Mr. and Mrs. Judson Dayton
Wayzata, Minnesota
(not pictured)

STUDY FOR STILL LIFE WITH NINE TULIPS
1983
14 × 20¾ inches
Evansville Museum of Arts & Science
Evansville, Indiana

STILL LIFE WITH TULIP, CHOCOLATE CHIPS, AND MARZIPAN
1983
47 × 35⅝ inches
Chemical Bank
New York

(overleaf)

STILL LIFE WITH PEARS AND CHERRIES
1983
40 × 29½ inches
M. Anwar Kamal, M.D.
Jacksonville, Florida

STILL LIFE LADEN WITH FRUIT
1984
40 × 60 inches
Jane and Stuart Weitzman
(*not pictured*)

STUDY FOR STILL LIFE LADEN WITH FRUIT
1984
14 × 21 inches
Mr. and Mrs. Donald B. Korb
Evansville, Indiana

STILL LIFE WITH MAD HATTER
1984
22 × 30 inches
Amerada Hess Corporation
New York

STILL LIFE WTH WATERMELON AND PALM
1984
60 × 40 inches
Transco Energy Company
Houston, Texas

FANCY CHOCOLATES AND BON BONS WITH CIGAR BOX
1985
12¾ × 12 inches
Mr. Remak Ramsay

(overleaf)

CHOCOLATE TRUFFLES AND HOKUSAI CARDS
1985
11½ × 11 inches each (diptych)
Mr. and Mrs. Ronald W. Moore
New York

2.
returned from him to
you though they were
mine before. If I
or she should chance
to be inv lved in
this affa he trusts
to you set them
free ex as we
were. Don let him
know she liked them
best for this must
ever be a secret
kept from all the rest
between yourself and
me.
J.

(overleaf)

COLONEL CHARLES DENBY'S DESK
1985
22 × 30 inches
Private Collection

STILL LIFE WITH DAGUERREOTYPES
1985
21½ × 16 inches
Mr. and Mrs. Eric M. Heiner
Charlottesville, Virginia

STILL LIFE WITH CANDYSTICKS
1985
20 × 14 inches
Mr. and Mrs. Sanford M. Besser
Little Rock, Arkansas

PETUNIAS AND WHITE COSMOS
1985
21½ × 24½ inches
Mr. and Mrs. Constantine Sidamon-Eristoff
New York

(overleaf)

STILL LIFE WITH PEONIES AND BUTTONS
1986
18 × 12 inches
Mr. and Mrs. Ronald W. Moore
New York

STILL LIFE WITH WALL PAINTING BASED ON KENSETT
1986
11⅜ × 19¾ inches
Mr. Peter W. May
New York

(overleaf)

STILL LIFE WITH LADYFINGERS AND CUNNINGHAM SUGAR BOWL
1986
18 × 12½ inches
Private Collection

Solo Exhibitions
Group Exhibitions
Selected Bibliography
Collections

EXHIBITIONS

Solo Exhibitions

1988
"The Eye and the Heart: Watercolors of John Stuart Ingle," Evansville Museum of
    Arts & Science, Evansville, Indiana (traveling exhibition)

1985
Tatistcheff Gallery, New York
Transco Energy Exhibition Gallery, Houston

1983
Tatistcheff Gallery, New York

1981
Tatistcheff Gallery, New York

1979
Capricorn Gallery, Bethesda, Maryland

1976
Southwest State University, Marshall, Minnesota

1975
Dana Art Center, Springfield, Massachusetts

Group Exhibitions

1987
"Still Life," Rahr-West Art Museum, Manitowoc, Wisconsin
"Six Realists," Harris Samuel & Company Gallery, Coconut Grove, Florida

1986
"Watercolor U.S.A. 1986: The Monumental Image," Springfield Art Museum,
    Springfield, Missouri
"Nature Morte," Southern Alleghenies Museum of Art, Loretto, Pennsylvania
"NYC: New Work," Delaware Art Museum, Wilmington, Delaware

1985
"American Realism: Twentieth-Century Drawings and Watercolors," San Francisco
    Museum of Modern Art
"American Painters: Figuration," Jane Haslem Gallery, Washington, D.C.
"Midwest Realists," Paine Art Center, Oshkosh, Wisconsin
"New American Scene," Squibb Gallery, Princeton, New Jersey
"Focus on Realism: Selections from the Collection of Glenn C. Janss,"
    The Boise Gallery of Art, Boise, Idaho
"The Recognizable Image," The Bruce Museum, Greenwich, Connecticut

1984
"Watercolors," Museum of Art, University of Arizona-Tucson (two-artist exhibition)
"Recent American Still Life," Robert Schoelkopf Gallery, New York
"Painting/Photography," Thorpe Intermedia Gallery, Sparkhill, New York
"Drawings, Drawings, Drawings," Forum Gallery, New York

1983

"Watercolor in America," University of Hartford, Hartford, Connecticut

"Painted Object Painted," Herbert Palmer Gallery, Los Angeles

"Realist Directions," Museum of Art, Pennsylvania State University, College Park

"Contemporary Images: Watercolor 1983," University of Wisconsin-Oshkosh

"Tulip Time," Impressions Gallery, Boston

"Twentieth-Century American Watercolor," The Gallery Association of New York State, Hamilton, New York (traveling exhibition)

"New American Watercolor," Frumkin/Struve Gallery, Chicago

"Realist Watercolors," Florida International University, Miami

"Do You See What I See?" Sawtooth Center of the Visual Arts, Winston-Salem, North Carolina

1982

"Perspectives on Contemporary American Realism: Works on Paper from the Collection of Richard and Jalene Davidson," The Pennsylvania Academy of the Fine Arts, Philadelphia, and The Art Institute of Chicago

"Every Object Rightly Seen," The University of Virginia, Charlottesville

1981

"Contemporary American Realism Since 1960," The Pennsylvania Academy of the Fine Arts, Philadelphia (traveling exhibition)

"Emphasis," Minneapolis Institute of the Arts (three-artist exhibition)

1980

"Ten Realist Views," Rutgers University, New Brunswick, New Jersey

"Watercolor 1980," Frumkin/Struve Gallery, Chicago

1977

Friends Gallery, Minneapolis Institute of the Arts

"Watercolor U.S.A.," Springfield Art Museum, Springfield, Missouri

1976

"Mainstream—1976," Marietta, Ohio

"2nd Annual Works on Paper Exhibition," Dana Art Center, Springfield, Massachusetts

"17th Red River Annual," Moorhead, Minnesota

1975

"1st Annual Works on Paper Exhibition," Dana Art Center, Springfield, Massachusetts

SELECTED BIBLIOGRAPHY

Periodicals

Baker, Kenneth. "New American Watercolors," *Portfolio,* September/October 1982, pp. 36-41.

Bolt, Thomas. "John Stuart Ingle," *Arts Magazine,* November 1985.

Camp, John. "Minnesota Painter's Star Brightest in Manhattan," *St. Paul Pioneer Press and Dispatch,* February 2, 1986.

Doherty, M. Stephen. "Watercolor Today," *American Artist,* February 1983, p. 86.

Donohoe, Victoria. "On Galleries," *The Philadelphia Inquirer,* June 1, 1985.

Driscoll, John Paul. "Paradigms of Reality," *American Artist,* March 1982, pp. 36-41 (cover).

Goodyear, Frank H., Jr. "American Realism Since 1960: Beyond the 'Perfect Green Pea,'" *Portfolio,* November/December 1981, p. 75.

Johnson, Patricia C. "Ingle's Watercolors: An Exhibit Not To Miss," *Houston Chronicle,* February 16, 1985.

Kramer, Hilton. "Critics' Choices," *The New York Times,* January 18, 1981.

Zimmer, William. "Realism Takes Over Greenwich's Bruce," *The New York Times,* February 17, 1985.

Exhibition Catalogues

Bolt, Thomas. "John Stuart Ingle." New York: Tatistcheff Gallery, 1985.

Goodyear, Frank H., Jr. "Perspectives on Contemporary American Realism." Philadelphia: Pennsylvania Academy of the Fine Arts, 1982.

Henry, Gerrit. "Realist Watercolors." Miami: Florida International University, 1983.

Kosinski, Dorothy M. "The Recognizable Image." Greenwich, Connecticut: The Bruce Museum, 1985.

Oresman, Janice. "Twentieth Century American Watercolor." Hamilton, New York: Gallery Association of New York State, 1983.

Books

Goodyear, Frank H., Jr. *Contemporary American Realism Since* 1960. Boston: New York Graphic Society, 1981, pp. 41, 155.

Martin, Alvin. *American Realism: Twentieth Century Drawings and Watercolors.* New York: Harry N. Abrams, Inc., 1986, pp. 51, 145, 150, 153, 157.

COLLECTIONS

Allied Bank of Texas, Houston
Amerada Hess Corporation, New York
American Express Company, New York
Arkansas Art Center, Little Rock
Becton Dickinson and Company, Paramus, New Jersey
Chemical Bank, New York
Citizen's National Bank, Evansville, Indiana
Crum & Forster Underwriters, Basking Ridge, New Jersey
Evansville Museum of Arts & Science, Evansville, Indiana
McCrory Corporation, New York
Metropolitan Life Insurance Company, New York
The Metropolitan Museum of Art, New York
NYNEX, New York
Pacific Bell, San Ramon, California
Philip Morris Companies, New York
The St. Paul Companies, St. Paul, Minnesota
Shearson/Lehman Brothers, New York
Southeast Banking Corporation, Miami
Stephens, Incorporated, Little Rock, Arkansas
Transco Energy Company, Houston
Triangle Industries, New York
Yale University Art Gallery, New Haven, Connecticut

1913106

759.1
INGLE

Ingle, John Stuart.

The eye and the heart

$30.00   rq

DATE			

© THE BAKER & TAYLOR CO.

01530 587873